Classic
ROSES
for Australian Gardens

JAMES YOUNG

cameron
HOUSE

Published by
Cameron House
An imprint of Bookwise International Pty Ltd
174 Cormack Road, Wingfield SA 5013, Australia

Produced for the publisher by
Murray David Publishing Pty Ltd
35 Borgnis Street, Davidson NSW 2085, Australia
With the assistance of Bernardi Martin, Adelaide, SA

First published 2002
Photographs, design and text © James Young 2002
Cover designed by Clare Forte
Text written, edited, designed and assembled by
    James Young
Digital colour separation and film by Typescan, Adelaide
Printed in Singapore

ISBN 1-875999-54-X

Acknowledgments

My thanks to Australia's foremost rosarian David Ruston
for his help in compiling this book. I have spent many
happy hours photographing his superb collection of roses
in Renmark, SA. My thanks also to Elwyn Swane for
allowing me to photograph the roses at Swane's
Nursery in Dural, NSW. Finally, I would like to thank
Murray Child and David Jenkins of Murray David
Publishing for their belief in me and this book, and
Gordon Cheers and Margaret Olds of Global Book
Publishing for encouraging me as a photographer.

Cover: 'First Love'
Previous page: 'Rosette Delizy'
Right: 'Chicago Peace'

Contents

For my mother
Margaret Jean

Introduction

AS LEGEND WOULD HAVE IT, around 600 BC the Greek poet Sappho named the rose 'Queen of Flowers' and to this day it is the world's favorite flower. None other is more admired, more cultivated or more loved.

The roses we know today have been derived, through centuries of breeding, from the wild roses. Wild roses grow in the temperate zones of the northern hemisphere. They are found in China and Japan, across Central Asia to North Africa and Europe, and in North America.

The early history of rose cultivation is lost in the mists of time. In fact, most of what we know of them comes from written records of the last 2500 years. The earliest records are from Greece, where roses were grown for their beauty and fragrance. The Greeks also knew how to extract rose oil, which was used on their persons and in cooking.

The Romans took over from the Greeks in their love of roses. Rose petals were strewn in the paths of heroes in triumphal processions and over tombs during funerals. They used garlands of roses to enhance orgies and feasts. In fact, the Roman emporer Elegabalus showered so many rose petals over his banqueting guests that several were suffocated. Roman legend has it that when Harpocrates discovered Venus in an illicit encounter, her son Cupid offered a rose in return for his vow of silence. Thus, the rose became a symbol of secrecy. Roses were probably introduced to England and France by the Romans. It was common in these countries for roses to be suspended over the dining table to remind guests that what they heard there was confidential, hence the origin of the term *sub rosa*, 'under the rose'.

At the fall of the Roman Empire, Europe went into the so-called Dark Ages. The

Previous page: 'Dove'
Right: 'Double Delight'

cultivation of roses fell into a decline during this period and hybrid roses owe their survival to their cultivation in monastries, mainly for medicinal purposes.

As Europe emerged from the Dark Ages, roses resumed their popularity, and by about 1700 there were five main groups of roses: these were the Gallicas, Damasks, Albas, Centifolias (which included Moss Roses) and Scots.

The most significant step in the breeding of modern roses was the introduction in the late eighteenth century of *Rosa chinensis* from China. Cross-breeding with this species brought the repeat-flowering characteristic to rose cultivars. Up until this time roses in the West usually flowered only once a year. Now they could flower repeatedly from early summer to late autumn. At the same time rose-breeding techniques were dramatically improving. Thus, in the early nineteenth century, many new varieties evolved: Noisettes, Bourbons, Hybrid Perpetuals, Boursaults, Portlands and the Teas.

Then, in 1867 came the Hybrid Teas (or Large-flowered Roses as they are also known). These roses were destined to strengthen the popularity of roses as never before. The first Hybrid Tea Rose was 'La France' bred by Jean-Baptiste Guillot of France. It was produced from a cross between a Hybrid Perpetual Rose and a Tea Rose, combining the vigor and hardiness of the former with the elegance and grace of the latter.

The birth of the Hybrid Tea Rose was so significant to rose breeders that the cut-off date between Old Garden Roses and Modern Garden Roses is considered by most to be the year 'La France' was introduced.

However, Hybrid Tea Roses lacked one important color—yellow. A French breeder, Joseph Pernet-Ducher, experimenting with a yellow rose introduced from the Middle East named 'Persian Yellow', managed to produce a repeat-flowering offspring from a cross between this rose and a red Hybrid Perpetual. He named this rose 'Soleil d'Or' and introduced it in 1900. This rose was actually yellow and red, but it since featured in the parentage of all of the early yellow Hybrid Tea Roses.

Another important development was the development of Floribunda Roses (also known as Cluster-flowered Roses) following World War I. To understand the origin of this class, we must go back to the crossing, by Guillot in 1875, of the China Rose 'Old Blush' with *Rosa multiflora,* a species that produced large clusters of flowers. A class of roses developed from this cross known as Polyantha Roses. These roses were resilient and hardy and they produced small flowers in clusters, providing a mass of color through summer. Then, the Dutch breeder Svend Poulsen started crossing Polyantha Roses with Hybrid Tea Roses, and the Floribunda Rose was born. It combined the beauty and elegance of Hybrid Tea Roses with the clustering, free-flowering characteristic of the Polyanthas.

These two classes—Hybrid Tea and Floribunda—account for the bulk of roses offered today.

Such was the popularity of Hybrid Tea and Floribunda Roses during the 1920s and '30s, that most of the Old Garden Rose varieties disappeared from rose catalogues. In fact, if it were not for the discernment of a number of rosarians who made it their business to scour old gardens and gather the rare Old Garden Roses into collections, very few would have survived. Fortunately, in the 1950s, Old Garden Roses came back into fashion and from these collections they have been reintroduced around the world. Sometimes these roses are referred to as Heritage Roses, and they are enjoying a resurgence in their popularity today.

The Old Garden Roses are tall and shrubby, with flowers that open wide. They are deeply cupped or in flat rosettes and most are

intensely fragrant. The color range is limited and most of them flower but once a year. In contrast Modern Garden Roses come in a dazzling array of colors. They have elegant, long, pointed buds that open to high-centered flowers, shiny green leaves and short, upright, disease-resistant growth. Most of them produce repeated flushes of flowers through the season. Unfortunately, although there are many Modern Garden Roses with good fragrance, none can compare with the richness of the scent of the Old Garden Roses.

An important development in recent times has been the work of David Austin in England, who has made it his goal to breed roses that combine the fragrance and charm of Old Garden Roses with the vigor, health, color range and repeat-flowering of the Moderns. So successful has he been that a sub-class of Modern Shrub Rose has developed, know as the English Rose.

Today there are some 25,000 rose varieties in cultivation and for the average rose fancier it can be a bit daunting deciding which ones to grow. In this book I have attempted to solve that problem by presenting the all-time classic one hundred roses for the average garden. All of the roses included here have proven their worth. They have been chosen for their popularity, their health, their ease of cultivation, their awards at rose shows, their easy availability and for their beauty and fragrance. The showstoppers from the last hundred years are all here, and a few from before that, and every one of the roses awarded World's Favourite Rose by the World Federation of Rose Societies is included. To top it all off, every rose is illustrated with a large, luscious picture. My intention was to not only make life easier for someone wanting to select and grow roses, but also to do justice to the Queen of Flowers.

Right: 'Mermaid'

Cultivation

MANY PEOPLE BELIEVE that roses are difficult to grow. This is a misconception, as roses are in fact surprisingly easy to cultivate and will perform reasonably well even if neglected. They will grow in a wide variety of positions, soils and climates, but for the best results a little care to create optimum conditions will pay dividends.

POSITION

Roses grow best in full sun; however, they will tolerate some shade. As a general rule roses require at least four hours of the day in sun. Any less than this and their performance suffers; expect to get fewer blooms and more spindly growth. Having said that, watch out for situations where your roses can get sunburnt. For instance, roses can burn it they are shaded for most of the day by buildings or fences and then get a burst of hot sun in the middle of the afternoon. Be wary of reflected heat from west-facing walls and fences. A protected corner with brick walls on two sides that gets the hottest sun of the afternoon is not the place for a rose, except perhaps as a potted specimen that can be moved somewhere else in the hottest part of summer.

Avoid cold, draughty spots, such as between the side of the house and the side fence, particularly if that area is also shady. On the other hand, avoid areas that are too protected from wind. Roses like to be ventilated and will suffer from fungus diseases in such situations.

The ideal position is out in the open. If the site is too windy, consider placing a windbreak to provide protection. A picket fence makes a better windbreak than a solid fence, which will create turbulence. A hedge, deciduous or otherwise, is ideal for this purpose.

Do not plant roses too close to large trees and shrubs whose roots will rob the soil of nutrients and water. Grow roses outside the dripline of such trees and shrubs.

SOIL

The best soil for roses is a rich, deep, crumbly loam that has plenty of decayed organic matter incorporated into it. However, roses will grow in a wide range of other soil types, especially if some effort is put into soil improvement.

It used to be thought that a clay soil was essential for rose growing, but this is not the case. Clay soils have a natural advantage in that they retain water and nutrients. But if the soil is high in clay it is important to dig it over to break it up and this can be hard work. The application of gypsum to heavy clay soils will, over time, help with this process.

It is important to know how well clay soil drains. Do not plant roses in areas that accumulate and hold water in wet weather, especially in winter. Such waterlogged areas need to have their drainage improved. The most effective way is to excavate and install underground drainage, but this is costly and takes hard work. A simpler way is to dig plenty of sand, gypsum and compost into the soil and raise the bed by 6–12 centimeters (2–5 inches) using a low retaining wall made of bricks or old railway sleepers.

If the soil is light and sandy then water and nutrients will drain too quickly through it. In such cases it is a good idea to introduce lots of organic matter into the soil in the form of manure and compost. A heavy layer of mulch in such situations will also help to retain moisture. Remember, lighter soils need lighter, but more frequent, feeding and watering.

Roses will grow in acid or alkaline soils provided they are not extreme. If it is suspected that the soil is extremely acid or alkaline then buy a soil-testing kit from the local garden center. The ideal pH for roses is between 6 and 6.5 (slightly acid), but in reality anywhere between 5.5 and 7.5 is okay. If the soil is very acid, the application of lime prior to planting will be beneficial. Conversely, if the soil is very

'Diamond Jubilee'

alkaline, the application of peat and manure will help rectify the situation. In extreme cases of alkalinity the application of sulphate of ammonia will be necessary.

Roses do not like to be planted on the site of an earlier rose garden. They will be slow to grow and will not thrive. It is believed that the decomposing roots of the old rose produce a growth inhibitor specific to roses. A remedy is to remove the top 35 centimeters (14 inches) of soil and replace it with good quality topsoil. The excavated soil can be used to grow other sorts of plants elsewhere without any worries.

Whatever the soil type it is important to prepare in advance the area where the roses are to be planted. Dig the area over thoroughly and incorporate plenty of organic matter. Do this by spreading compost or old manure over the top of the soil to a depth of about 6 centimeters (2 inches) — more or less depending on the amount of organic matter already in the soil. Then, dig the organic matter in to the depth of the garden fork. Don't expect to do the preparation and planting in one day. Let everything settle for a few weeks before planting. Don't overdo it with organic matter or the rose will not be able to anchor itself properly. Let common sense prevail.

PLANTING

There are two ways in which roses are usually sold: in a pot or bare rooted. Make sure to buy the best quality available. Beware of low price tags, they often mean stunted, badly shaped plants.

If the rose comes bare rooted, dig a hole deep enough to accommodate the roots. Partly fill the hole with well broken up soil and place the plant in the hole so that the bud union will be just above the soil level. Fill the hole with soil, packing it well around the roots. Tamp the soil down firmly leaving a slight depression around the rose. Fill this with water a couple of times and let the water soak away. Then add a generous layer of mulch. Take care to leave the stem free of mulch so that the micro-organisms that break down the mulch do not attack the delicate bark.

If the rose comes in a pot, simply dig a hole a bit deeper than the pot requires. Place a small amount of broken up soil in the bottom of the hole, then tip the rose out of its container. Place it in the hole, making sure that the top of the pot soil is level with the top of the hole. Fill around the rootball with the soil you dug out to make the hole and tamp it firmly in place. Water thoroughly and mulch it as described above. Do not fertilize at planting time unless it is with a slow-release fertilizer. Ordinary fertilizers will burn the new roots as they grow.

MULCHING

Roses love to be mulched. Mulches help retain moisture, prevent weeds and add organic matter to the soil as they break down. Dead leaves, lawn clippings, well-rotted manure, seaweed, pine chips, lucerne hay and straw all make good mulches. Spread the mulch over the surface to a depth of 10 centimeters (4 inches) and replace it as it rots away. Keep the mulch free of the rose stem to prevent it from becoming part of the decomposition process.

WATERING

Roses are deep-rooted plants and their water needs are straightforward. They like deep watering to encourage deep roots. Light watering will encourage surface roots and the rose will not withstand dry periods very well. In hot summer weather a good soak every week is all that is required. In spring and autumn, increase the period between waterings to fortnightly. Always bear in mind how much rain has fallen and compensate for it. Lighter, sandy soils need a lighter watering two or three times more frequently than loamy soils.

It is better to apply the water at ground level to prevent fungus diseases. A soaker hose upside down is perfect for this. Drip irrigation systems are also good; run them for twenty-four hours at each watering.

If growing roses in containers they will need watering daily in hot weather.

FERTILIZING

Roses need regular feeding because they put so much energy into flower production. Organic matter, such as rotted manure or compost, regularly incorporated into the soil three times a year is ideal: at pruning time in winter; after spring flowering; and in late summer to encourage autumn flowers. The addition of a reputable brand of rose fertilizer at this time is also beneficial. Follow the instruction on the packet. Don't be tempted to mix it stronger. More is not always better.

DEADHEADING

If spent flowers are left on the bush it devotes its energy to hips and seeds. Deadheading encourages more blooms. Latest research suggests that the dead flower should be removed at the swollen section of the stem below the flower where the first leaflets are found. Snap off the stem with the fingers. Deadhead right through the season for maximum flower production.

PRUNING

Many people believe that pruning roses is a
complicated and difficult art. However, this is a
misconception; rose pruning requires just a
little knowledge and some common sense.

There are two main reasons to prune: to
control the size and neatness of the bush; and
to maximize flower production. The best time
to prune is in late winter or early spring. In
cold climates this should be done when any
danger of frost has passed, so that the new
shoots do not get frostbitten.

'Just Joey'

Roses are constantly renewing themselves by
producing strong new watershoots from the
base. These will be seen as very fresh, healthy
looking shoots that emerge from the bud union.
(The bud union is the lumpy thing at the base
of the plant, just above the ground. It is the
place where the rose has been grafted onto the
understock.) These watershoots have a
lifecycle: they produce good flowers for a
season or two; then they start to lose their
vigor; and then they eventually die. The object
of pruning is to accelerate this process, by
removing the ageing shoots, so that the energy
of plant can be concentrated in the new.

The necessary tools for pruning include a good pair of secateurs, a small pruning saw to cut branches that are too thick for the secateurs and heavy gloves to protect the hands.

Here are some guidelines for pruning Bush Roses, the most commonly grown class:

- Remove any dead wood right at the base with secateurs or a pruning saw.
- Remove any spindly, untidy or sickly shoots at the base.
- Remove the oldest branch at the base and any other shoots that have not produced good flowers for a while, especially where they are near strong new shoots.
- Remove any branches that cross others and produce crowding.
- Remove any shoots that come from below the bud union, as these are suckers; they come from the understock and are not desirable. They are easy to identify because they have a different sort of leaf to that of the main plant.
- Shorten the remaining shoots by one-third to one-half of their length. Make these shortening cuts at an angle to the stem just above a prominent eye or axil bud (found in the leaf axil). Choose an eye or bud that is facing outward or towards an open space in the bush and make sure the eye looks strong, healthy and promising. Remember, the harder the pruning the larger but fewer will be the resultant flowers. Less severe pruning will result in smaller and more numerous flowers.

Shrub Roses and Old Garden Roses need less pruning than Bush Roses. In fact, they need no pruning for the first four or five years, apart from occasionally removing an old or dead stem. Alternatively, they can be pruned as for Bush Roses for a more restrained result.

Climbing Roses and Ramblers need different treatment, as follows:

- Remove the dead and diseased wood. Also, remove the older unproductive shoots that are three or four years old.
- Find new stems to replace the ones that have have been removed and tie them into position. Be gentle with the canes, they can snap easily.
- Cut the side shoots off the main stems to buds or eyes. Leave these side stems no longer than about 6–8 centimeters (2–3 inches).
- Cut the main stems to the first side shoot, which will then take over as leader.
- Rearrange the remaining stems and tie them down to evenly cover the support. If the rose is growing over a wall or fence, try to have the main long stems arranged horizontally along the support. Do not bend any canes below horizontal—they won't grow 'downhill'. If the rose is growing on a pillar or arch, spiral the main stems around the support.

Groundcover Roses need no pruning at all except to keep them within bounds.

PESTS AND DISEASES

Healthy roses are better able to resist pests and diseases. If the plant has good soil, is in the right situation and is well-fed and watered, then it should have fewer problems. Remember also that not all roses are created equal. Some will do better than others in the same conditions. If one variety is not doing well, remove it and try another. Most of the roses presented in this book have a proven record of reliability and resistance to pests and diseases.

PESTS

Aphids. These are tiny, soft, green or brown sap-sucking insects that cluster on the soft tips and buds of the rose. They can be physically removed by squashing between finger and thumb. Or they can be dislodged by using a high-speed jet of water from a hose. For severe infestations use a pyrethrum-based insecticide.

Remember, insecticides can kill the natural predators of aphids such as ladybugs. Make some enquiries at the garden center, there are some that are selective.

Spider mites. These occur in hot, dry weather. They cause a bronzing on the upper surfaces of the leaves, making the foliage look dry. Look under the leaves and there will be fine web, and a magnifying glass will reveal lots of tiny insects and eggs. The best remedy is to put a spinkler under the bushes to wet the undersides of the leaves.

Thrips. These appear as tiny, winged insects that blow in with warm winds. They seem to prefer lighter colored blooms, where they appear as mobile, dark slivers. They leave the blooms bruised and lack-lustre. Because they are very difficult to control the best thing with thrips is to just wait until they go away. Spray them if you must with neem oil or a systemic insecticide.

'Julia's Rose'

Scale. These are insects that attach themselves to the older stems of the plant. They appear as flat, waxy disks. If the infestation is minor you can remove them by hand. Spraying with a mixture of half-strength malathion and half-strength white oil will kill them.

Caterpillars. These chew the leaves, giving a skeletal appearance, or they bore into the buds. The best way to control them is pick them off by hand. If the infestation is severe ask at the garden center for the name of a product that is a specific biological control for caterpillars.

DISEASES

Black spot. This, along with powdery mildew, is by far the most common problem with roses. It appears as random black spots on the foliage and if untreated it will result in defoliation of the rose and loss of vigor. Black spot thrives in high humidity and warmth and is generally more of a problem in coastal areas. Prevention is better than cure, so in humid climates it is a good idea to commence spraying in early spring with a good brand of rose fungicide from the garden center. Spray regularly at two-week intervals throughout the season.

Powdery mildew. This occurs in fine, mild weather when there is overnight dew. It appears as a powdery bloom on the young shoots and leaves. Treatment is by spraying with an appropriate fungicide, available from the garden center. Conveniently, many of the sprays available for black spot are also appropriate for mildew. Always read the labels carefully for specific instructions.

Rust. This is quite a serious disease, but fortunately not as common as black spot and mildew. It appears as small rusty looking specks on the backs of the leaves with corresponding light green spots on their tops. At the first sign of rust you must act quickly. Consult your garden center for a product that will deal with rust and spray as instructed on the label.

Classification of Roses

There are various systems of classification of roses and they all have their merit. Some suit the hybridist, while others are more relevant to exhibitors. The World Federation of Rose Societies adopted a system in 1979. The classification system used here is a simplification of that system.

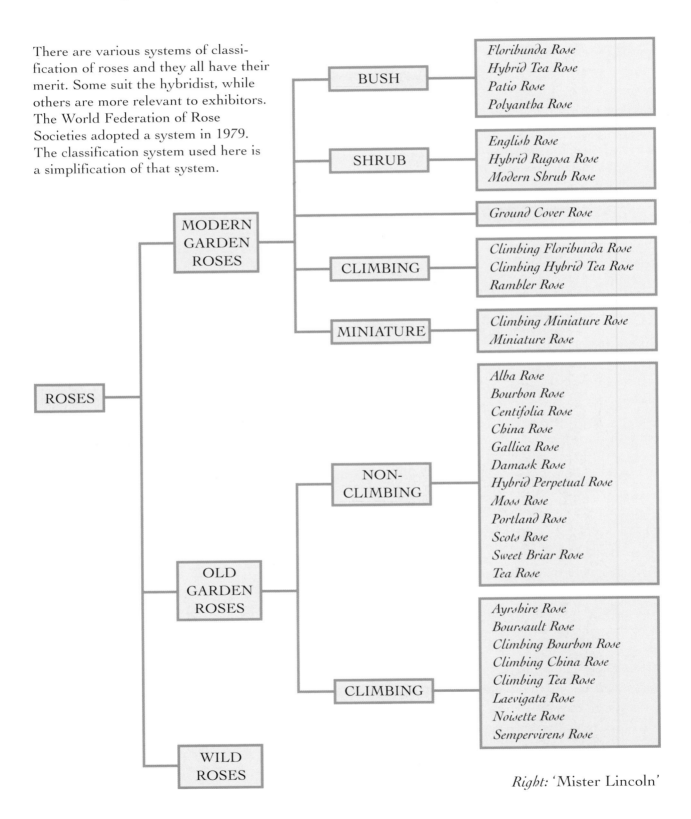

ROSES

MODERN GARDEN ROSES

- **BUSH**
  - Floribunda Rose
  - Hybrid Tea Rose
  - Patio Rose
  - Polyantha Rose
- **SHRUB**
  - English Rose
  - Hybrid Rugosa Rose
  - Modern Shrub Rose
- Ground Cover Rose
- **CLIMBING**
  - Climbing Floribunda Rose
  - Climbing Hybrid Tea Rose
  - Rambler Rose
- **MINIATURE**
  - Climbing Miniature Rose
  - Miniature Rose

OLD GARDEN ROSES

- **NON-CLIMBING**
  - Alba Rose
  - Bourbon Rose
  - Centifolia Rose
  - China Rose
  - Gallica Rose
  - Damask Rose
  - Hybrid Perpetual Rose
  - Moss Rose
  - Portland Rose
  - Scots Rose
  - Sweet Briar Rose
  - Tea Rose
- **CLIMBING**
  - Ayrshire Rose
  - Boursault Rose
  - Climbing Bourbon Rose
  - Climbing China Rose
  - Climbing Tea Rose
  - Laevigata Rose
  - Noisette Rose
  - Sempervirens Rose

WILD ROSES

Right: 'Mister Lincoln'

Classic Roses

'Abraham Darby'

Named for a pioneering English Industrialist of the eighteenth century, this rose bears large, very double, cup-shaped flowers in small clusters. The color is a peach-apricot pink and there is a strong fruity fragrance. Flower production is wonderfully profuse in spring but not so good in autumn. The foliage is dark green and shiny and the plant is bushy and very vigorous, forming a large arching shrub. It can also be trained as a pillar or a small climber.

Codename: AUScot
Synonyms: 'Abraham', 'Country Darby'
Classification: English Rose
Breeder: Austin, England
Year of introduction: 1985
Parentage: 'Aloha' × 'Yellow Cushion'
Fragrance: Strong
Repeat flowering

'Anvil Sparks'

Often grown for its novelty value, with blooms in a most unusual concoction of orange-red, striped and stippled in yellow, this rose is not the most easy to grow. If you have ideal conditions for roses (a warm dry climate and good soil conditions) by all means grow it, but be warned it is not the most robust of bushes and in humid areas it suffers badly from black spot. Apart from these drawbacks it bears most striking, fragrant blooms from elegant buds. This rose is a sport (or mutation) of another and was discovered in a garden in East London, South Africa.

Synonyms: 'Amboss Funken', 'Ambossfunken'
Classification: Hybrid Tea
Breeder: Meyer, South Africa
Year of introduction: 1961
Parentage: Sport of 'Signora Piero Puricelli'
Fragrance: Strong
Repeat flowering

'Apricot Nectar'

This rose is excellent for cutting, as the blooms last well, especially if cut when still in bud. The very large flowers are up to 13 cm (5 in) across. They are a magnificent shade of pink-apricot, with a yellow base to the petals. A popular rose for many years, 'Apricot Nectar' has a strong fruity fragrance and bears profuse clusters of flowers through summer and autumn. It is a good idea to remove some of the buds in the clusters to prevent overcrowding. There is plenty of glossy, dark green foliage and the growth is bushy and vigorous. In fact, it can make an excellent bushy standard if so grafted. 'Apricot Nectar' won the All-America Rose Selection in 1966.

Classification: Floribunda
Breeder: Boerner, USA
Year of introduction: 1965
Parentage: Seedling × 'Spartan'
Fragrance: Strong
Repeat flowering

'Belle Story'

This is a beautifully fragrant rose, with large, light pink, cupped, double flowers. They open to reveal that the bases of the petals blend to yellow and there are prominent red-gold stamens. The petals incurve towards the center in the manner of some of the old Hybrid Perpetuals. Foliage is medium green and semi-glossy and the growth is vigorous, bushy and branching. 'Belle Story' was named for one of the first nursing sisters to serve as a British Royal Navy officer.

Codenames: AUSelle, AUSspry
Synonym: 'Bienenweide'
Classification: English Rose
Breeder: Austin, England
Year of introduction: 1984
Parentage: ('Chaucer' × 'Parade') ×
  ('The Prioress' × 'Iceberg')
Fragrance: Yes
Summer flowering

'Blue Moon'

This is the most popular of the so-called 'blue' roses. Although scientists are working hard to graft blue genes into roses, the closest we have to blue in the rose world are roses like 'Blue Moon', that are slightly on the blue side of lilac. Long, pointed buds open to large, very full, delightfully fragrant flowers on long stems. They are good for cutting, lasting well in the vase. The foliage is dark green and the growth is vigorous. There is also a climbing version available known as 'Climbing Blue Moon'. 'Blue Moon' won Anerkannte Deutsche Rose and a Gold Medal in Rome in 1964.

Codename: TANnacht
Synonyms: 'Blue Monday', 'Mainzer Fastnacht', 'Sissi'
Classification: Hybrid Tea
Breeder: Tantau, Germany
Year of introduction: 1965
Parentage: 'Sterling Silver' seedling × seedling
Fragrance: Strong
Repeat flowering

'Bonica'

This is a firm favorite rose with many growers due the abundance of its flowers and the health of the bush. The color is a clear pink and the repeat is quick and generous, so that it always seems to be covered in masses of small, cupped lightly fragrant flowers from spring through until autumn. The bright green foliage is most attractive and it is a low grower, making it ideal for group plantings in landscape display.

Codename: MEIdomonac
Synonyms: 'Bonica 82', 'Bonica Meidiland', 'Demon'
Classification: Floribunda
Breeder: Meilland, France
Year of introduction: 1981
Parentage: (*Rosa sempervirens* × 'Mlle Marthe Carron') × 'Picasso'
Fragrance: Light
Repeat flowering

Brass Band

Fat orange-yellow buds open to very full-petaled flowers in a strong brassy orange, blended with various shades of pink. There is a light fragrance. The flowers are most attractive when they first open, but they can fade to a less attractive gray-green color as they age. Flowering in quite large clusters the flowers are particularly bright and well shaped in the cooler autumn weather, which brings out more apricot colors in the flowers. It is a low, bushy grower and has plenty of bright green foliage, which contrasts well with the strong colors of the flowers.

Codename: JACcofl
Classification: Floribunda
Breeder: Christensen, USA
Year of introduction: 1994
Parentage: 'Gold Badge' × seedling
Fragrance: Light
Repeat flowering

'Buff Beauty'

This rose is quite a pale buff color in the spring but the color deepens in the autumn to apricot yellow. There is a strong fragrance and it has plenty of shiny, dark green leaves. It is probably one of the most sprawling roses found in gardens, making it excellent for growing over rockeries or training on low walls. It makes a graceful rounded shrub. Excellent as a pillar rose, the blooms come on short arms and hang downwards, so that one looks up at the flowers. It is healthy and disease free.

Classification: Modern Shrub
Breeder: Bentall, England
Year of introduction: 1939
Parentage: 'William Allen Richardson' × seedling
Fragrance: Strong
Repeat flowering

'Candella'

This is an elegant rose from the New Zealand breeder Sam McGredy. The petals are rich crimson on the inside and silvery white on the outside, giving a most striking effect. There are very few roses in this color combination. The fully double flowers open from long, pointed buds and are of medium size with high centers. The foliage is large, dark green and semi-glossy and the growth is vigorous, tall and upright.

Codename: MACspeego
Synonym: 'Eternally Yours'
Classification: Hybrid Tea
Breeder: McGredy, NZ
Year of introduction: 1990
Parentage: 'Howard Morrison' × 'Esmeralda'
Fragrance: Light
Repeat flowering

'Charles Austin'

This is a remarkable rose, bearing masses of flowers in a delightful apricot, tinged with pink. The flowers fade to light pink as they age and they are packed with petals in a well-shaped, cupped rosette. There is a strong fruity fragrance. The foliage is medium green and dense and there are plenty of hooked red prickles. Its one drawback is that repeat flowering can be unreliable; apply fertilizer and give it a heavy trim after the first flush to encourage later blooms. It is named for the breeder's father.

Codenames: AUSles, AUSfather
Classification: English Rose
Breeder: Austin, England
Year of introduction: 1973
Parentage: 'Chaucer' × 'Aloha'
Fragrance: Strong
Repeat flowering

'Chaucer'

David Austin named many of his roses after
characters from Chaucer's *The Canterbury Tales*.
This one is named for the poet himself.
Released in 1970, this is one of the earliest of
the English Roses. Light pink, deeply cupped
flowers are borne in clusters from globular
buds. They show a hint of stamens. The
fragrance is very strong and fruity. Foliage is
medium green and matt and there are lots of
red prickles. Growth is upright and bushy and
the flowering is more or less continuous
through the season.

Codenames: AUScer, AUScon
Classification: English Rose
Breeder: Austin, England
Year of introduction: 1970
Parentage: 'Duchesse de Montebello' ×
    'Constance Spry'
Fragrance: Strong
Repeat flowering

'Chicago Peace'

This is a sport (or mutation) from 'Peace' that first occurred in a garden in Chicago, hence the name. 'Chicago Peace' is perhaps even more striking than 'Peace', having bright pink flowers with a strong yellow base. The effect is intense and luminous. The flowers are large, high-centered, and lightly fragrant. As the flowers age they become pleasantly ruffled. The foliage is very dark green, leathery and glossy and the growth is vigorous, tall and bushy. 'Chicago Peace' won a Gold Medal at Portland in 1962. There is also a climbing version available known as 'Climbing Chicago Peace', but it is not a very prolific bloomer.

Codename: JOHnago
Classification: Hybrid Tea
Breeder: Johnston, USA
Year of introduction: 1962
Parentage: Sport of 'Peace'
Fragrance: Light
Repeat flowering

'Claire Rose'

One of the earlier introductions of David Austin, it is also one the best. The blooms are a particularly soft, pure pink, with an apricot blush in the centre. They are very full and of rosette shape and there is a strong fragrance. The gray-green foliage is closely jointed and very attractive, which suggests it might have an Alba Rose somewhere in its parentage. It forms a large bush 2–3 m (6–10 ft) in height, is very healthy and disease resistant, flowering well through the season.

Codename: AUSlight
Classification: English Rose
Breeder: Austin, England
Year of introduction: 1986
Parentage: 'Charles Austin' × (seedling × 'Iceberg')
Fragrance: Strong
Repeat flowering

'Colorama'

This rose, from the French breeder Meilland, is an unusual combination of red mixed with yellow. Oval buds open to high-centered flowers of exhibition form that hold well on the bush and in the vase. It is very free flowering and there is a pleasant fragrance. The foliage is a dark, glossy green on an upright and bushy plant. Healthy and disease resistant, 'Colorama' is an excellent garden rose. Repeat is quick and abundant.

Codename: MEIrigalu
Synonyms: 'Colourama', 'Dr R. Maag'
Classification: Hybrid Tea
Breeder: Meilland, France
Year of introduction: 1968
Parentage: 'Suspense' × 'Confidence'
Fragrance: Strong
Repeat flowering

'Complicata'

This rose grows much taller than most Gallicas, producing huge, arching sprays that cascade downwards. It has very attractive large, flat, single, bright pink flowers with golden stamens. It produces a good crop of hips but does not flower after the first flush. Many growers have reported that it grows well in shady areas, particularly under deciduous trees where it can get away to a good start before the trees get their leaves. There is plenty of gray-green foliage and the bush is very healthy.

Synonyms: 'Ariana d'Algier', *Rosa gallica complicata*
Classification: Gallica
Breeder: Unknown
Year of introduction: Unknown (pre-1800)
Parentage: Unknown
Fragrance: Yes
Summer flowering

'Crépuscule'

'Crépuscule' is a Noisette Rose. These roses are great for hot climates because there they are evergreen and everblooming from spring, through summer to early winter. The sweetly fragrant flowers have about 20 petals in a strong apricot color and they come in small clusters. This is a versatile rose performing well as a climber, shrub, pillar or weeping standard. The foliage is very abundant, with few thorns, and the bush is very healthy. *Crépuscule* is the French word for twilight.

Classification: Noisette
Breeder: Dubreuil, France
Year of introduction: 1904
Parentage: Unknown
Fragrance: Strong
Repeat flowering

'Diamond Jubilee'

Well-shaped, ovoid buds open to buff-yellow to light apricot flowers. They are double, cupped and large, up to 15 cm (6 in) across. Winner of the All-America Rose Selection in 1948 and a Royal National Rose Society award in 1952, it is fragrant and the foliage is leathery and olive green. Growth is vigorous and upright. 'Diamond Jubilee' has been widely grown and exhibited in rose shows for over fifty years and remains popular to this day.

Classification: Hybrid Tea
Breeder: Boerner, USA
Year of introduction: 1947
Parentage: 'Maréchal Niel' × 'Feu Pernet-Ducher'
Fragrance: Yes
Repeat flowering

'Dr Grill'

A lot of controversy surrounds this rose. There are four or five different roses in various collections around the world, from Sanger-hausen in Germany to great gardens in France and America, claiming the name and the credentials of 'Dr Grill'. The version seen here is arguably the best. It is a lightly tea fragrant, very full-petaled concoction of soft cream with a mauve-pink edge to each petal. It holds its bloom very well and the bush is almost thornless, growing to 2 m (7 ft), flowering well through the season. In warm climates it flowers sporadically right through winter.

Synonyms: 'Doctor Grill', 'Docteur Grill', 'Dulce Bella'
Classification: Tea
Breeder: Bonnaire, France
Year of introduction: 1887
Parentage: 'Ophirie' × 'Souvenir de Victor Hugo'
Fragrance: Light
Repeat flowering

'Dolly Parton'

This is a voluptuous rose named for a voluptuous woman. It has large, double, full, luminous orange-red flowers with a heavy fragrance. It is unusual for a rose of this color to have such good fragrance; no doubt it inherits this characteristic from its impeccable parentage. The foliage is medium green and glossy, bronze-red when young. The growth is upright, bushy and moderately vigorous.

Classification: Hybrid Tea
Breeder: Winchel, USA
Year of introduction: 1983
Parentage: 'Fragrant Cloud' × 'Oklahoma'
Fragrance: Strong
Repeat flowering

'Double Delight'

This is an striking and unusual rose, a bit gaudy for some. The buds are long and pointed to urn shaped, opening to very large blooms that are creamy white in the center, becoming strawberry red on the outside with exposure to the sun. Winning many awards, including the All-America Rose Selection in 1977, Gold Medals at Baden-Baden and Rome in 1976 and the Gamble Medal for Fragrance in 1986, it is exceedingly popular to this day. In 1985 it was named World's Favourite Rose. The foliage is matt and mid-green and the growth is upright, bushy and spreading. There is a climbing form available that repeats well.

Codename: ANDeli
Classification: Hybrid Tea
Breeder: Swim & Ellis, USA
Year of introduction: 1977
Parentage: 'Granada' × 'Garden Party'
Fragrance: Strong
Repeat flowering

'Dove'

'Dove' bears masses of delicate, light pink, double, cupped flowers of at least 40 petals. It repeats well and has a light apple fragrance. The foliage is medium sized, dark green, glossy and disease resistant. Growth is vigorous and spreading. It makes a good standard and because of its low growth and bushiness it excellent as a bedding rose or grafted into a standard.

Codename: AUSdove
Synonym: 'Dovedale'
Classification: English Rose
Breeder: Austin, England
Year of introduction: 1984
Parentage: 'Wife of Bath' × 'Iceberg' seedling
Fragrance: Light
Repeat flowering

'Duet

This a well-named rose as the tops of the petals are light pink and the bottoms of the petals are a darker pink, giving an unmistakable and enchanting effect. It is very free flowering in clusters of three to five and it repeats very quickly giving great continuity to a most attractive rose. Foliage is plentiful and healthy and the bush is medium in height. It grows easily from cuttings. It won the All-America Rose Selection in 1961 and numerous other awards around that time. All in all, this is a 'must-have' rose.

Classification: Hybrid Tea
Breeder: Swim, USA
Year of introduction: 1960
Parentage: 'Fandango' × 'Roundelay'
Fragrance: Light
Repeat flowering

'First Love'

'First Love' is one of the earliest pink roses to flower. Small, refined, well-shaped buds open to well-shaped, mildly fragrant blooms in a lovely combination of soft pink edged with deep pink. It is of very bushy habit, practically thornless and the foliage is pale green. Its one fault is that older plants never seem to produce much basal wood, making them appear a little gaunt. In spite of that it still flowers very well, repeating nicely through the season.

Synonym: 'Premier Amour'
Classification: Hybrid Tea
Breeder: Swim, USA
Year of introduction: 1951
Parentage: 'Charlotte Armstrong' × 'Showgirl'
Fragrance: Light
Repeat flowering

'Fragrant Cloud'

This rose has won many awards and enjoyed great popularity since its introduction. Ovoid buds open to large, well-formed, double, coral red flowers that fade slightly as they age. They are intensely fragrant and the foliage is dark green and glossy. The growth is vigorous and upright. Awards include the Gamble Fragrance Medal in 1969, Gold Medals from the Royal National Rose Society in 1963 and Portland in 1967, and in 1981 the World Federation of Rose Societies declared it World's Favourite Rose. There is also a climbing version available known as 'Climbing Fragrant Cloud'.

Codename: TANellis
Synonyms: 'Duftwolke', 'Nuage Parfumé'
Classification: Hybrid Tea
Breeder: Tantau, Germany
Year of introduction: 1963
Parentage: Seedling × 'Prima Ballerina'
Fragrance: Strong
Repeat flowering

'Frau Dagmar Hartopp'

This is the smallest of the so-called Hybrid Rugosas, derived from *Rosa rugosa* that grows wild near the seashores of Japan. 'Frau Dagmar' has the most delicate, pale silvery pink flowers, with cream stamens, followed by huge, tomato red hips that are often mixed with the last of the flowers. If it is planted with the bud union below the ground it will sucker into quite a thicket. It is a very vigorous, disease-resistant and trouble-free plant, lending itself to landscape planting, and has lots of rich green foliage. The Royal Horticultural Society gave this rose an Award of Merit in 1993.

Synonyms: 'Dagmar Hastrup', 'Frau Dagmar Hastrup', 'Fru Dagmar Hastrup'
Classification: Hybrid Rugosa
Breeder: Hastrup, Denmark
Year of introduction: 1914
Parentage: Unknown
Fragrance: Light
Repeat flowering

'Friesia'

If you are looking for a yellow Floribunda Rose with fragrance, this is the rose to choose. Ovoid buds open to large, double, rich yellow, very fragrant flowers that fade slightly as they age. The foliage is mid-green and shiny and the bush is vigorous and upright. Repeat flowering is excellent and the old blooms shatter quickly leaving the bush looking neat and tidy. 'Friesia' has been rewarded with the Baden-Baden Gold Medal in 1972, the James Alexander Gamble Fragrance Award in 1979 and the James Mason Medal in 1989.

Codename: KOResia
Synonym: 'Sunsprite'
Classification: Floribunda
Breeder: Kordes, Germany
Year of introduction: 1977
Parentage: Seedling × 'Spanish Sun'
Fragrance: Strong
Repeat flowering

'Gold Bunny'

This is one the best yellow Floribundas, as a bush rose, standard or climber. The bush form grows as wide as it is tall. The climber form is restrained, to about 3 m (6 ft), and it repeats well. The mildly fragrant flowers are borne in clusters of three to seven and they are of a particularly clear shade of yellow that fades to only a slightly paler yellow with age. It is one of the first Floribundas to flower in the spring and repeat flowering is rapid and abundant. The foliage is dark green and glossy and some-what susceptible to black spot in cooler climates.

Codename: MEIgronura
Synonyms: 'Gold Badge', 'Rimosa '79'
Classification: Floribunda
Breeder: Paolino, France
Year of introduction: 1978
Parentage: 'Poppy Flash' × ('Charleston' × 'Allgold')
Fragrance: Light
Repeat flowering

'Gold Medal'

This is a classically shaped rose with deep golden yellow, double flowers, sometimes flushed orange and light red. The hotter the weather the deeper the color. The high-centered blooms open from long, ovoid, pointed, spiraled buds. There is a light, fruity, tea fragrance. The foliage is large and dark green and the plant is tall, upright and bushy. The repeat is very quick and there are very few thorns. This is a very good yellow rose for warm climates often flowering well into winter.

Codename: AROyqueli
Synonym: 'Golden Medal'
Classification: Hybrid Tea
Breeder: Christensen, USA
Year of introduction: 1982
Parentage: 'Yellow Pages' × ('Granada' × 'Garden Party')
Fragrance: Light
Repeat flowering

'Hannah Gordon'

Classed as a Hybrid Tea in some circles and a Floribunda in others, the large flowers come in small clusters on a very strong bush. The lightly fragrant blooms are very pale pink flushed with deepest pink on the edges of the petals. With only around 14 petals the flowers have an arresting simplicity. Of roses in this color it is perhaps the most elegant. Foliage is dark green and abundant. The Royal National Rose Society gave a Trial Ground Certificate in 1983.

Codename: KORweiso
Synonyms: 'Raspberry Ice'
Classification: Floribunda
Breeder: Kordes
Year of introduction: 1983
Parentage: Seedling × 'Bordure Rose'
Fragrance: Light
Repeat flowering

'Heritage'

This rose has double, cupped, medium-sized, light pink blooms in small to medium clusters. They are full of petals, which incurve toward the center of the flower in the style of Old Garden Roses. The blooms are borne from fat buds and have a strong fragrance. The foliage is small, mid-green and semi-glossy. Growth is upright and bushy. 'Heritage' flowers freely all season and is good for cutting or garden display. It can also make a good hedge.

Codename: AUSblush
Synonym: 'Roberta'
Classification: English Rose
Breeder: Austin, England
Year of introduction: 1984
Parentage: Seedling × ('Wife of Bath' × 'Iceberg')
Fragrance: Strong
Repeat flowering

'Iceberg'

This is probably the most widely grown rose of all time. It is good for landscaping, due to the attractiveness of the robust bush and the generosity of its flowers. It covers itself all through the season in repeated flushes of semi-double, very dainty, shapely white blooms in large and small clusters. The flowers are rain-resistant and long lasting. The color is pure white, except in cooler weather when they can be touched with palest pink. The foliage is light green and glossy and extremely disease resistant. 'Iceberg' makes a good standard and there is a climbing version, 'Climbing Iceberg', which has the same disease resistance and generosity of bloom. 'Iceberg' won Gold Medals from the Royal National Rose Society and at Baden-Baden in 1958. It was World's Favourite Rose in 1983 and won the Royal Horticultural Society Award of Merit in 1993.

Codename: KORbin
Synonyms: 'Fée des Neiges', 'Schneewittchen'
Classification: Floribunda
Breeder: Kordes, Germany
Year of introduction: 1958
Parentage: 'Robin Hood' × 'Virgo'
Fragrance: Light
Repeat flowering

'Jacquenetta'

This English Rose has fallen out of favor with the breeder in recent years due to the fact that it does not repeat well. A heavy trimming after the first flush and application of fertilizer at this time will encourage later blooms. Despite this, it is a rose of great charm. It has cupped, ruffled, light apricot flowers, showing prominent yellow stamens. The foliage is dark green and semi-glossy and there is a light fragrance.

Codename: AUSjac
Synonym: 'Jaquenetta'
Classification: English Rose
Breeder: Austin, England
Year of introduction: 1983
Parentage: Unknown
Fragrance: Light
Repeat flowering

'Joyfulness'

One of the best Hybrid Teas to be introduced in the last thirty years, 'Joyfulness' is a lovely combination of peach, cream and soft apricot. The flowers are well shaped on a strong healthy bush. It repeats well and the blooms hold well in the vase. There is a climbing form known as 'Climbing Joyfulness' that doesn't grow too large and retains the good repeat-flowering characteristics of the parent, making it one of the few really good apricot climbers. There is plenty of glossy, dark green foliage but watch out for black spot. It won a Royal National Rose Society Certificate of Merit in 1963.

Codename: TANsinnroh
Synonyms: 'Frohsinn 82', 'Peccato di Giola'
Classification: Hybrid Tea
Breeder: Tantau, Germany
Year of introduction: 1982
Parentage: Unknown
Fragrance: Light
Repeat flowering

'Julia's Rose'

Although not the easiest rose to grow, 'Julia's Rose' is very popular for its unique color—a mixture of coffee, parchment and copper shades—making it very handsome in flower arrangements. Small, pointed buds on short stems open to small, slightly fragrant, double flowers. The foliage is olive green, tinted reddish, and the growth is upright. It was named for the acclaimed flower arranger, Julia Clements, and took the floral art world by storm on its introduction. It needs protection from fungus diseases and the best in terms of soil and feeding. It won a Gold Medal at Baden-Baden in 1983.

Classification: Hybrid Tea
Breeder: Wisbech, England
Year of introduction: 1976
Parentage: 'Blue Moon' × 'Dr A. J. Verhage
Fragrance: Slight
Repeat flowering

'Just Joey'

'Just Joey' is just magnificent—a photograph cannot convey the size of the blooms. With classically shaped, double, buff-orange flowers, almost the size of cabbages, 'Just Joey' also has a heavy scent. The blooms last well on the bush and in the vase. Very popular since its introduction, 'Just Joey' will remain a favorite indefinitely. It has glossy and leathery foliage and the bush is sprawling and moderately vigorous. This rose has won many awards, including the Royal National Rose Society James Mason Gold Medal in 1986, the Royal Horticultural Society Award of Garden Merit in 1993 and World's Favourite Rose in 1994.

Classification: Hybrid Tea
Breeder: Cant, England
Year of introduction: 1972
Parentage: 'Fragrant Cloud' × 'Dr A. J. Verhage'
Fragrance: Strong
Repeat flowering

'Kardinal'

'Kardinal' has long been a popular florists' rose, for its long stems, vivid color and light fragrance. It is also a good performer in the garden, with its vigorous, compact growth and disease resistance. The flowers are a rich bright red and are well shaped, high centered and of perfect form for exhibition. This is one of the first roses to flower in the garden and it repeats quickly. The stems are very thorny, an inheritance from its parent 'Flamingo'.

Codename: KORlingo
Classification: Hybrid Tea
Breeder: Kordes, Germany
Year of introduction: 1986
Parentage: Seedling × 'Flamingo'
Fragrance: Light
Repeat flowering

'Lamarque'

This is one of the greatest of the Noisette Roses. It has evergreen foliage and after a good spring showing it flowers sporadically through summer to a good display in autumn. The large, very full, very quartered flowers come in small clusters. The color is cream with a slightly yellowish center that looks well against the abundant green foliage and it has a good fragrance. It grows nicely on pergolas and arches and is an excellent climber to grow among the branches of a small tree like an apple or cherry.

Synonyms: 'Général Lamarque', 'La Marck', 'Thé Maréchal'
Classification: Noisette
Breeder: Maréchal, France
Year of introduction: 1830
Parentage: 'Blush Noisette' × 'Parks' Yellow Tea-scented China'
Fragrance: Strong
Repeat flowering

'Lilian Austin'

Yet another rose from the prolific breeder David Austin, and this time he named the rose in honor of his mother, which means he must have thought it very special. In fact, it is the only English Rose that comes in quite this color. It has globular buds that open to wide, informal, double, salmon pink blooms, borne in clusters of one to five and has plenty of fragrance. The foliage is a glossy dark green. It has hooked, brown prickles and strong, low, spreading growth, making it eminently suitable for the front of a border, where it will spill over a path.

Classification: English Rose
Breeder: Austin, England
Year of introduction: 1973
Parentage: 'Aloha' × 'The Yeoman'
Fragrance: Strong
Repeat flowering

'Limelight'

An amazingly colored rose that produces well-shaped, yellow buds with a hint of lime, on long stems. They open to soft yellow flowers flushed with green. The flower is most attractive when it is a half to three-quarters open. There is good fragrance and the bush is healthy and covered in plenty of dark green, glossy foliage. The flowers hold their color well when picked. Its one fault is that it can be susceptible to mildew.

Codename: KORikon
Synonym: 'Golden Medallion'
Classification: Hybrid Tea
Breeder: Kordes, Germany
Year of introduction: 1985
Parentage: 'Peach Melba' × seedling
Fragrance: Strong
Repeat flowering

'Lolita'

This is a very tall growing rose producing single flowers on stems as long as 1 m (3 ft). The very large, perfectly formed flowers are a wonderful, soft apricot-peach. They open to very full blooms with petals incurving towards their centers much in the style of peonies. It is a fairly thorny, free-flowering, trouble-free rose, having plenty of healthy, bronze green foliage. 'Lolita' won Annerkante Deutsche Rose in 1973.

Codenames: KORlita, litaKOR
Classification: Hybrid Tea
Breeder: Kordes
Year of introduction: 1973
Parentage: 'Colour Wonder' × seedling
Fragrance: Strong
Repeat flowering

'Madam President'

This is a most beautiful rose that looks its best when a half to three-quarters open, the lightly fragrant flowers resembling formal camellias. The color is a very soft pale pink with a cream base to the petals. They are borne in happy profusion on a short well-foliaged bush that is trouble free and repeats quickly. Not as widely known and loved outside of Australia and New Zealand as it should be, it is an outstanding rose, and well worth growing.

Synonym: 'Madame President'
Classification: Floribunda
Breeder: McGredy, New Zealand
Year of introduction: 1975
Parentage: Seedling × 'Handel'
Fragrance: Light
Repeat flowering

'Margaret Merril'

This is a very popular rose in cool climates. The large and plentiful foliage is very dark green, almost thornless. The large, semi-double, high-centered, white flowers, shading to creamy buff in the center, open slowly and have great substance. The bush is very vigorous and healthy and the repeat is very quick. It is a rose that will suit both hot and cold climates. There is a strong citrus fragrance. It has won awards to numerous to mention.

Codename: HARkuly
Synonym: 'Margaret Merrill'
Classification: Floridunda
Breeder: Harkness
Year of introduction: 1978
Parentage: ('Rudolph Timm' × 'Dedication') × 'Pascali'
Fragrance: Strong
Repeat flowering

'Mary Rose'

This is one of the favorite English Roses of the raiser, David Austin, who named it to mark the occasion of the raising of Henry VIII's flagship *Mary Rose* from the Solent, after it had been underwater for more than 400 years. The flowers are double, very cupped, fragrant and a delightful shade of medium pink. The petals drop rather quickly, but the prolific production of flowers means this rose is spectacular for much of the season. The foliage is medium sized, mid-green and matt and the growth is vigorous, upright and bushy. Two sports of 'Mary Rose' have been registered: the pale pink 'Redouté' and the almost blush 'Winchester Cathedral'.

Codename: AUSmary
Classification: English Rose
Breeder: Austin, England
Year of introduction: 1983
Parentage: Seedling × 'The Friar'
Fragrance: Yes
Repeat flowering

'Mermaid'

'Mermaid' is extremely vigorous—in warmer climates it can literally cover a house. Distinctively pointed buds open to large, single flowers in a creamy yellow, flushed darker in the center, with amber stamens. Foliage is dark and glossy and it is viciously thorny. It is useful to cover an old shed or other unsightly feature.

Classification: Miscellaneous Old Garden Rose
Breeder: Paul, England
Year of introduction: 1918
Parentage: Rosa bracteata × a Tea Rose
Fragrance: Yes
Repeat flowering

'Mister Lincoln'

Winner of the All-America Rose Selection in 1965, this has remained a favorite red rose to this day. And no wonder. Single, large, urn-shaped buds on long stems open to large, double, high-centered, dark velvety red flowers. No one can resist their beauty and the fragrance is magnificent. The foliage is dark green and leathery and the growth vigorous and disease resistant. It is a very tall grower, to 3.5 m (12 ft), so it looks best at the back of the bed or border. There is also a climbing version known as 'Climbing Mister Lincoln'.

Classification: Hybrid Tea
Breeder: Swim & Weeks, USA
Year of introduction: 1964
Parentage: 'Chrysler Imperial' × 'Charles Mallerin'
Fragrance: Strong
Repeat flowering

'Mrs Oakley Fisher'

This is one of the three great single Hybrid Tea Roses, the others being 'White Wings' and 'Dainty Bess'. Orange buds open to luscious, fragrant, apricot flowers, set off by prominent red-gold stamens and abundant, healthy, bronze foliage. The flowers fade as they age but retain their charm. They come in clusters on somewhat spindly looking stems, and for this reason many growers keep it trimmed to a low bushy shape rather than hoping for full Hybrid Tea form. It won a Royal National Rose Society Certificate of Merit in 1921 and a Royal Horticultural Society Award of Garden Merit in 1993.

Classification: Hybrid Tea
Breeder: Cant, England
Year of introduction: 1921
Parentage: Unknown
Fragrance: Strong
Repeat flowering

'Monsieur Tillier'

There is a lot of controversy about this Tea Rose, which is grown worldwide by rose lovers and mostly in the form seen here. Peter Beales in England has introduced another rose of the same name, which he claims is the true 'Monsieur Tillier', quite a different rose. Leaving all that aside, this is a lovely Tea Rose in a combination of various shades of pink, fading to salmon in the center. It is a very variable rose in the number of petals, there being far fewer petals in the heat of the summer than in the cooler weather. In hot climates it hits its prime in the late autumn and winter months. It is strongly fragrant.

Synonym: 'Archduc Joseph'
Classification: Tea
Breeder: Bernaix, France
Year of introduction: 1891
Parentage: Unknown
Fragrance: Strong
Repeat flowering

'Mutabilis'

The origins of this rose are somewhat of a mystery. Apparently growing in the garden of an Italian Prince at Isola Bella, he presented it to Henri Correvon of Geneva, who re-introduced it to horticulture in 1934. Many think it originally came from China. The name means 'changeable' and refers to the changing color of the flowers. Salmon buds open to single, mildly fragrant, salmon flowers, which slowly flush from pink through to red. A bush in full flower looks as if it is covered in butterflies, hence its alternative name 'Butterfly Rose'. In hot climates it can grow 2–3 m (6–9 ft) high and wide. It is a healthy rose with few problems.

Synonyms: 'Butterfly Rose', *Rosa chinensis mutabilis, R. turkestanica*, 'Tipo Idéale'
Classification: China
Breeder: Unknown
Year of introduction: Unknown (pre-1894)
Parentage: Unknown
Fragrance: Light
Repeat flowering

'New Dawn'

This is one of the best climbers in regard to its quick and abundant repeat-flowering characteristics. With its long trailing growth it also makes an excellent weeping standard. The small, strongly fragrant, double flowers are a particularly soft, clear pink. It is fairly thorny, has good disease-free foliage and has remained a firm favorite of rose growers since its introduction. In 1993 it won a Royal Horticultural Society Award of Garden Merit and in 1997 it was awarded World's Favourite Rose, being the first climber to be so honored.

Synonyms: 'Everblooming Dr W. van Fleet',
  'The New Dawn'
Classification: Climbing Hybrid Tea
Breeder: Somerset Rose Nursery
Year of introduction: 1930
Parentage: Sport of 'Dr W. van Fleet'
Fragrance: Strong
Repeat flowering

'Olé'

Very popular in the United States, this rose has well-shaped buds that open to medium-sized, luminous, bright orange-red flowers, that are ruffled and high centered. There are at least 50 petals and the overall effect is striking. Lasting well in the vase, the blooms have good fragrance. The foliage is very glossy and mid-green and the bush is vigorous and disease resistant. 'Olé' is a good rose to provide a bright splash of color in the garden, but be careful it doesn't clash with other bright colors.

Classification: Hybrid Tea
Breeder: Armstrong, USA
Year of introduction: 1964
Parentage: 'Roundelay' × 'El Capitan'
Fragrance: Yes
Repeat flowering

'Our Vanilla'

Belonging to a group of roses informally known as 'parchment roses', the petals are indeed reminiscent of old paper. The color is an unusual creamy white with a green tinge. The flowers hold well in the vase but like many roses with stiff petals there is no scent, vanilla or otherwise. Foliage is bright green and leathery and the bush is healthy. It is a rose more suited to warm climates or a greenhouse.

Codename: KORplasina
Synonym: Vanilla
Classification: Floribunda
Breeder: Kordes, Germany
Year of introduction: 1994
Parentage: Unknown
Fragrance: None
Repeat flowering

'Papa Meilland'

Produced singly, on long stems, the handsome, pointed buds open to large, double, high-centered, deep velvety crimson flowers. There is a heady fragrance. All of these characteristics ensured that it would become a favorite florists' rose, and no doubt it has sealed the pact for countless lovers. The foliage is leathery, glossy and mid-green and the growth is vigorous, tall and upright. Its one drawback is a tendency to develop mildew and black spot, so fungicides are a must in humid areas. 'Papa Meilland' was named for the raiser's grandfather and won the Baden-Baden Gold Medal in 1962 and the

Gamble Fragrance Medal in 1974. In 1988 it was voted World's Favourite Rose. There is a climbing version available called 'Climbing Papa Meilland', which is rather a gaunt grower.

Codenames: MEIsar, MEIcesar
Classification: Hybrid Tea
Breeder: Meilland, France
Year of introduction: 1963
Parentage: 'Chrysler Imperial' × 'Charles Mallerin'
Fragrance: Strong
Repeat flowering

'Paradise'

This is an eye-catching rose due to its color combination. Long, pointed buds open to large, double, well-formed, silvery lavender flowers that shade to ruby red at the edges. It is also known as 'Burning Sky', which is rather apt. For those who enjoy mauve roses this is a 'must-have'. To top it all off, there is good fragrance. The foliage is dark green and glossy and the growth is upright and vigorous. 'Paradise' won the All-America Rose Selection in 1979 and a Gold Medal at Portland in that same year. Its one fault is that young foliage is prone to burn badly in hot summers.

Codename: WEZeip
Synonym: 'Burning Sky'
Classification: Hybrid Tea
Breeder: Weeks, USA
Year of introduction: 1978
Parentage: 'Swarthmore' × seedling
Fragrance: Yes
Repeat flowering

'Pascali'

This is probably the most popular white Hybrid Tea, due to its formal beauty and outstanding performance. Long stems carry cream buds that open to medium-sized, creamy white, well-formed, double flowers. There is little or no fragrance. The foliage is dark green and the growth is vigorous, bushy and disease resistant. 'Pascali' was acclaimed on its introduction and won numerous awards, including Golden Rose of The Hague and the Royal National Rose Society Certificate of Merit in 1963, the Gold Medal at Portland in 1967, the All-America Rose Selection in 1969, and was inducted into the World Federation of Rose Societies Hall of Fame in 1991 as World's Favourite Rose.

Codename: LENip
Synonym: 'Blanche Pascal'
Classification: Hybrid Tea
Breeder: Lens, Belgium
Year of introduction: 1963
Parentage: 'Queen Elizabeth' × 'White Butterfly'
Fragrance: Slight
Repeat flowering

'Peace'

Many consider this to be the rose of the century. It has won numerous awards, including, among others, the Portland Gold Medal in 1944, the All-America Rose Selection in 1946, Golden Rose of The Hague in 1965 and World's Favourite Rose in 1976. The flowers are large, high-centered, fragrant and golden yellow, edged rose pink. It was raised during World War II and was named to mark the end of that conflict. The foliage is dark green, leathery and glossy and the growth is vigorous, tall and bushy. There is also a climbing version available.

Synonyms: 'Béke', 'Fredsrosen', 'Goia', 'Gloria Dei', 'Mme A. Meilland'
Classification: Hybrid Tea
Breeder: Meilland, France
Year of introduction: 1944
Parentage: (['George Dickson' × 'Souvenir de Claudius Pernet'] × ['Joanna Hill' × 'Charles P. Kilham']) × 'Margaret McGredy'
Fragrance: Yes
Repeat flowering

'Perdita'

The large, very full-petaled, cupped, soft blush-apricot flowers are borne in small clusters and they are very fragrant. The foliage is medium sized, medium green and semi-glossy and the growth is bushy and of medium height, to 1 m (3 ft), making it an excellent bedding rose. The repeat bloom is quick and abundant. 'Perdita' won the Edland Fragrance Medal in 1984. It was named for the heroine of Shakespeare's *A Winter's Tale*.

Codename: AUSperd
Classification: English Rose
Breeder: Austin, England
Year of introduction: 1983
Parentage: 'The Friar' × (seedling × 'Iceberg')
Fragrance: Strong
Repeat flowering

'Perfect Moment'

Winner of the All-America Rose Selection in 1991, this is another rose with dramatically contrasting colors, in the style of 'Double Delight'. Pointed buds, in well-shaped clusters, open to medium-sized, double, cupped, high-centered blooms that are yellow in the centre and red on the outer edges. There is light fragrance. The foliage is medium sized, mid-green and semi-glossy. Growth is upright, bushy and vigorous, to medium height. The color contrast is greater in warm climates.

Codename: KORwilma
Synonym: 'Jack Dayson'
Classification: Hybrid Tea
Breeder: Kordes, Germany
Year of introduction: 1989
Parentage: 'New Day' × seedling
Fragrance: Light
Repeat flowering

'Peter Frankenfeld'

Well-shaped buds open to large, double, high-centered, deep rose pink flowers of exhibition form. They are borne on long stems and last well in the vase, making them ideal for cutting. The fragrance is only light, which is probably why this rose did not win awards following its introduction. The foliage is dark green and matt and the growth is vigorous and bushy. It was named for a German comedian. It is a very useful rose as it flowers early and repeats quickly. There is a climbing version available called 'Climbing Peter Frankenfeld', which is a somewhat sparse producer of blooms.

Classification: Hybrid Tea
Breeder: Kordes, Germany
Year of introduction: 1966
Parentage: 'Ballet' × 'Florex'
Fragrance: Light
Repeat flowering

'Pink Peace'

With 'Peace' as a grandparent on both sides, it is no wonder this rose is a beauty. The flowers are large, full of petals, double and well shaped. They are of a particularly striking shade of dusty pink and are very fragrant. The color is not to everyone's taste and it can be difficult to co-ordinate with other colors. Nevertheless, it is an impressive sight when in full bloom. The foliage is leathery, mid-green and matt and the growth is vigorous, tall and bushy. There is a climbing sport available called 'Climbing Pink Peace', although it may be difficult to find. 'Pink Peace' won Gold Medals in Geneva and Rome in 1959.

Codename: MEIbil
Classification: Hybrid Tea
Breeder: Meilland, France
Year of introduction: 1959
Parentage: ('Peace' × 'Monique') × ('Peace' × 'Mrs John Lang')
Fragrance: Strong
Repeat flowering

'Princess Margaret of England'

Named for the Queen of England's late sister, this rose has 'Queen Elizabeth' as its seed parent and 'Peace' as one of its grandparents. It bears large, double, high-centered, phlox pink flowers. There is a light fragrance. The foliage is leathery and dark green and the growth is vigorous and upright. It won the Portland Gold Medal in 1977. There is also a climbing version available that is popular called 'Climbing Princess Margaret of England', which is a sparse producer of blooms and very upright in growth.

Codenames: MEIlista, MEIlisia
Synonym: 'Princesse Margaret d'Angleterre'
Classification: Hybrid Tea
Breeder: Meilland, France
Year of introduction: 1968
Parentage: 'Queen Elizabeth' × ('Peace' × 'Michèle Meilland')
Fragrance: Light
Repeat flowering

'Princesse de Monaco'

This rose was named for the screen goddess Grace Kelly, who married a handsome prince and lived happily ever after—until her untimely death from a car accident. It is another rose with 'Peace' in its parentage, this time as pollen parent. The large, very fragrant, double, high-centered flowers are cream, edged with pink. They are borne on long stems and are of exhibition form. The foliage is large, dark green and glossy and the growth is upright and bushy. Repeat blooming is very good. The climbing form, 'Climbing Grace de Monaco', also flowers freely over a long period.

Codename: MEImagarmic
Synonyms: 'Grace Kelly', 'Preference', 'Princess of Monaco', 'Princesse Grace', 'Princesse Grace de Monaco'
Classification: Hybrid Tea
Breeder: Meilland, France
Year of introduction: 1982
Parentage: 'Ambassador' × 'Peace'
Fragrance: Strong
Repeat flowering

'Pristine'

This is one of America's most popular exhibition roses. The pale pink flowers have excellent form and come on very long stems. Disease resistant, dark green foliage sets the flowers off well. The flowers open quite quickly, but are very beautiful in the bud stage. It is quite thorny and has a mild fragrance. In 1979 'Pristine' won both the Gold Medal at Portland and the Royal National Rose Society Edland Fragrance Medal.

Codename: JACpico
Classification: Hybrid Tea
Breeder: Warriner, USA
Year of introduction: 1978
Parentage: 'White Masterpiece' × 'First Prize'
Fragrance: Light
Repeat flowering

'Prospero'

This is not an easy rose to grow as it lacks vigor. However, many people take the trouble to grow it because it is so captivating. Mid-sized, deep crimson blooms that age to purple are borne freely through the season. They are quartered in the old style and richly fragrant. 'Prospero' requires regular feeding and spraying against disease to give of its best. Its beauty comes at a cost—it is very thorny.

Codename: AUSpero
Classification: English Rose
Breeder: Austin, England
Year of introduction: 1982
Parentage: 'The Knight' × 'Château de Clos Vougeot'
Fragrance: Strong
Repeat flowering

'Queen Elizabeth'

This rose caused quite a sensation when it was introduced and has remained popular ever since. Long, pointed buds open to large, double, high-centered, medium pink flowers. There is a light fragrance. The foliage is dark green, glossy and leathery and the growth is very tall, upright and bushy. It was named after the present Queen of England and introduced in honor of her ascent to the throne. Winner of awards too numerous to mention, suffice it to say that in 1979 it was voted World's Favourite Rose. There is also a climbing version available that is very vigorous, but does not repeat well.

Synonyms: 'Queen of England', 'The Queen Elizabeth Rose'
Classification: Floribunda
Breeder: Lammerts, USA
Year of introduction: 1954
Parentage: 'Charlotte Armstrong' × 'Floradora'
Fragrance: Light
Repeat flowering

'Radio Times'

The name commemorates the seventieth anniversary of the publication of the English magazine *Radio Times*. The flowers come in small clusters and they are large, very double, flat and rosetted in the Old Garden Rose style, and they come in a deliciously soft rose pink. They have a strong fragrance. The foliage is dark green and semi-glossy and the growth is vigorous and spreading. A fairly recent English Rose introduction, it is also among the best.

With its low growth it is suitable for small gardens and in the front of a border.

Codename: AUSsal
Classification: English Rose
Breeder: Austin, England
Year of introduction: 1994
Parentage: Unknown
Fragrance: Strong
Repeat flowering

'Red Gold'

Large clusters of elegant buds open to shapely, double, fragrant flowers in gold, tinged with a red edge. Growth is upright, with plenty of healthy dark green foliage. A very free-flowering rose, it continues well into the autumn. The blooms last well in the vase. It won a Royal National Rose Society Certificate of Merit in 1966, the Gold Medal at Portland in 1969 and the All-America Rose Selection in 1971.

Codename: DICor
Synonyms: 'Alinka', 'Redgold', 'Rouge et Or'
Classification: Floribunda
Breeder: Dickson, Ireland
Year of introduction: 1971
Parentage: ('Karl Herbst' × 'Masquerade') × 'Faust'
Fragrance: Light
Repeat flowering

'Redouté'

This rose is named after the artist Pierre-Joseph Redouté, who left a legacy of beautiful rose illustrations. These were painted while under the patronage of Empress Joséphine Bonaparte of France, a great lover of roses. The flowers are large, double, cupped and soft pink. There is a light fragrance. The foliage is medium green and matt and the growth is vigorous, bushy and disease resistant. 'Redouté' is popular among gardeners due to its prolific flower production, lovely flower shape and soft pink color. It makes an excellent bedding rose.

Codename: AUSpale
Classification: English Rose
Breeder: Austin, England
Year of introduction: 1992
Parentage: Sport of 'Mary Rose'
Fragrance: Yes
Repeat flowering

'Rosette Delizy'

This is one of last of the Tea Roses to be introduced, in the 1920s. It was the 'Double Delight' of its day, a rose in a startling blend of colors. The flowers are coppery yellow in the center, blending to apricot salmon, heavily overlaid with pink and red on the outer petals. This is particularly pronounced in the cooler weather. The buds are shapely and the full-blown flowers are full of petals. It repeats well and has a light tea fragrance.

Classification: Tea
Breeder: Nabonnand, France
Year of introduction: 1922
Parentage: 'Général Galliéni' × 'Comtesse Bardi'
Fragrance: Light
Repeat flowering

'Royal Dane'

Copper-apricot shaded to red on the outer petals is the color of the shapely, high-centered flowers, which open from refined buds on very long stems. It is a good rose for cutting, lasting lasting well in the vase and there is strong fragrance. The foliage is closely jointed, healthy and abundant. It is very free flowering over a long period and is a good background rose for a border.

Codename: POUmidor
Synonym: 'Troika'
Classification: Hybrid Tea
Breeder: Poulsen, Denmark
Year of introduction: 1971
Parentage: ('Tropicana' × ['Baccará' × 'Princesse Astrid']) × 'Hanne'
Fragrance: Strong
Repeat flowering

'Royal Highness'

One of the best roses from the 1960s, 'Royal Highness' has remained popular due to its many qualities. Classic urn-shaped buds open to well-formed, high-centered blooms in a very pleasing pale pink, the color deepening in warmer climates. Foliage is very glossy and dark green. The stems are longer in the cooler weather. Keep an eye out for black spot and mildew to which it can be prone. Repeat is very quick and there is a strong tea fragrance. 'Royal Highness' won the Gold Medal at Portland in 1969, the Madrid Gold Medal in 1962 and the All-America Rose Selection in 1963.

Synonyms: 'Konigliche Hoheit', 'Königlicht Hoheit'
Classification: Hybrid Tea
Breeder: Herbert, USA
Year of introduction: 1962
Parentage: 'Virgo' × 'Peace'
Fragrance: Strong
Repeat flowering

95

'St Cecilia'

The flowers are pale blush-pink, fading to creamy pink as they age. They are medium sized, double, deeply cupped and have a rich myrrh fragrance. The foliage is small, medium green and matt. There are small brown prickles. The growth is bushy and low, making it suitable for the front of a border or in a small garden. 'St Cecilia' comes into flower after most of the other English Roses are finished, making it useful as a provider of continuing color.

Codename: AUSmit
Synonym: 'St Cecelia'
Classification: English Rose
Breeder: Austin, England
Year of introduction: 1987
Parentage: Unknown
Fragrance: Strong
Repeat flowering

'St Patrick'

The urn-shaped buds open to brilliant, golden yellow, double, high-centered flowers of exhibition form. The outer petals of the flowers are touched with green. The colors are better in the hotter months. The foliage is medium green and semi-glossy and the growth is upright, bushy and disease-resistant. Repeat is quick and abundant. With a spotless pedigree, 'St Patrick' won the All-America Rose Selection in 1996.

Codename: WEKamanda
Classification: Hybrid Tea
Breeder: Strickland
Year of introduction: 1995
Parentage: 'Brandy' × 'Gold Medal'
Fragrance: None
Repeat flowering

'Sally Holmes'

One of the best of the Modern Shrubs, 'Sally Holmes' forms a massive bush up to 3–4 m (10–13 ft) high and almost as wide. In spring it bears huge panicles of coppery buff buds that open to pure white, 5-petaled flowers, with a boss of golden stamens. There are up to 60 blooms per panicle. A bush in full flower is quite a spectacle. It flowers after the first flush of main roses and repeats well through the season. 'Sally Holmes' won a Royal National Rose Society Trial Ground Certificate in 1975, the Belfast Certificate of Merit in 1979, the Baden-Baden Gold Medal in 1980, the Glasgow Fragrance Award in 1993 and the Portland Gold Medal in the same year.

Classification: Modern Shrub
Breeder: Robert A. Holmes, England
Year of introduction: 1976
Parentage: 'Ivory Fashion' × 'Ballerina'
Fragrance: Light
Repeat flowering

'Scabrosa'

This is a very good selected form of *Rosa rugosa*. The flowers are velvety purple in great abundance, with creamy stamens. Each flower forms a huge tomato red hip, that ripens at Christmas in the Southern Hemisphere, where the hips are sometimes used as a substitute for holly. The flowers continue to form among the hips in quite a startling display. Foliage is typically rugose and exquisite, coloring brilliant golden orange in the late autumn before falling. Planted with the bud union below the ground it will sucker into a thicket. 'Scabrosa' won a Royal Horticultural Society Award of Garden Merit in 1993.

Synonyms: *Rosa rugosa scabrosa*, *R. r.* 'Superba'
Classification: Hybrid Rugosa
Breeder: Harkness, England
Year of introduction: 1950
Parentage: Unknown
Fragrance: Strong
Repeat flowering

'Seduction'

Beautifully formed soft pink buds open to softest pink flowers with a cream base, which slowly fade to a paler pink. It is at its best in spring and autumn in hot climates, because the hot summer sun bleaches too much color from the flowers. The bushes are as wide as they are high, making it ideally suited to growing as a standard and repeat is quick and abundant. There is plenty of healthy green foliage, but no scent. 'Seduction' won Gold Medals at the Bagatelle and Courtrai in 1987.

Codename: MEIbeausai
Synonyms: 'Charles Aznavour', 'Matilda', 'Pearl of Bedfordview'
Classification: Floribunda
Breeder: Meilland, France
Year of introduction: 1988
Parentage: MEIgurami × 'Nirvana'
Fragrance: None
Repeat flowering

'Sexy Rexy'

Despite its somewhat bawdy name this rose bears huge clusters of delightful, delicate, medium pink, shapely flowers. A bush in full flower is a sight indeed, but sadly it is sometimes slow to repeat. Despite this it has become a firm favorite. There is a light fragrance. The foliage is small, light green and glossy and the growth is compact, bushy and disease resistant. 'Sexy Rexy' has won a swag of awards, including the the Royal National Rose Society Certificate of Merit in 1985, Gold Medals at Glasgow in 1989 and Portland in 1990, the Royal Horticultural Society Award of Garden Merit in 1993 and the Royal National Rose Society James Mason Gold Medal in 1996.

Codename: MACrexy
Synonym: 'Heckenzauber'
Classification: Floribunda
Breeder: McGredy, NZ
Year of introduction: 1984
Parentage: 'Seaspray' × 'Dreaming'
Fragrance: Light
Repeat flowering

'Shady Lady'

This rose is well named as it is one of the few roses that will tolerate quite a lot shade, although it will always do better in full sun. The semi-double, pink flowers come in very large, open trusses amid abundant soft green foliage. Flower production is good right through the season. Alas, there is no fragrance. The bush is tall and bushy, more suited to the back of a border or several can be planted to make a tall hedge.

Codename: MEIsecaso, MEIxtraflo
Synonym: 'Lutin'
Classification: Modern Shrub
Breeder: Meilland, France
Year of introduction: 1987
Parentage: Unknown
Fragrance: None
Repeat flowering

'Sharifa Asma'

One of David Austin's favorites, this rose was named for a member of the royal family of Oman. The shell pink, very double flowers open cupped, then become flat and rosetted like an Old Garden Rose. The flowers have a very appealing translucent quality. There is a sweet fragrance touched with myrrh. The foliage is medium green and disease resistant and the growth is short, upright and bushy.

Codename: AUSreef
Synonym: 'Sharifa'
Classification: English Rose
Breeder: Austin, England
Year of introduction: 1989
Parentage: 'Mary Rose' × 'Admired Miranda'
Fragrance: Yes
Repeat flowering

'Sombreuil'

This is a beautiful, old-fashioned Climbing Tea Rose, perfect for a pillar or growing over a pergola as it is not too strong in growth and it flowers right through the season. The creamy white flowers have delicate old-world charm, packed with petals, with a quartered center and there is a strong tea fragrance. It is healthy and disease resistant and has been a firm favorite for 150 years and is found in many old American colonial gardens.

Synonyms: 'Colonial White', 'Madame de Sombreuil', 'Mlle de Sombreuil'
Classification: Climbing Tea
Breeder: Robert, France
Year of introduction: 1850
Parentage: Seedling of 'Gigantesque'
Fragrance: Strong
Repeat flowering

'Sonia'

Long buds open to large, double, high-centered, pink flowers, which are suffused with coral to yellow. They are borne singly on long stems, making 'Sonia' a good florists' rose; in fact, it is probably the most popular of all greenhouse roses. There is a strong, fruity fragrance. The foliage is dark green, glossy and leathery and the growth is tall, upright and bushy. It was named for Francis Meilland's daughter. There is a good repeat-flowering climbing form available.

Codename: MEIhelvet
Synonym: 'Sonia Meilland', 'Sweet Promise'
Classification: Hybrid Tea
Breeder: Meilland, France
Year of introduction: 1974
Parentage: 'Zambra' × ('Baccará' × 'White Knight')
Fragrance: Strong
Repeat flowering

'Souvenir d'Elise Vardon'

Like most Teas, this rose flowers over a long period. It is very bushy in growth, as wide as it is tall, and is quite thorny, with abundant disease-free foliage. The flowers can be variable in size, number of petals and color depending on the season. It reaches peak production in the late autumn and early winter in warm climates. Nice buds open to strongly fragrant, quartered flowers, full of petals, in a wonderful concoction of rosy pink, fawns and creams. It is one of the great surviving Tea Roses from the past.

Synonym: 'Souvenir d'Elisa Vardon'
Classification: Tea
Breeder: Marest, France
Year of introduction: 1854
Parentage: Unknown
Fragrance: Strong
Repeat flowering

'Souvenir de la Malmaison'

Popular for more than 150 years, this is one of the best of the Bourbons. The flowers are very elegant—cupped, packed with petals, and quartered in the center—and the color is an indescribably delicate shade of pink. The bush form is quite small, up to 1 m (3 ft) but there is a climbing form available that is very strong. 'Souvenir de la Malmaison' revels in dry climates, but the buds tend to ball in wet climates. In warm climates the climbing form can flower right through the winter.

Synonym: 'Queen of Beauty and Fragrance'
Classification: Bourbon
Breeder: Béluze, France
Year of introduction: 1843
Parentage: 'Mme Desprez' × a Tea Rose
Fragrance: Strong
Repeat flowering

'Souvenir de Mme Léonnie Viennot'

This rose can be very variable in color, but is usually a combination of various shades of pink with a yellow base to the petals. It can be quite rosy pink or it can be apricot pink. It doesn't need much pruning because it flowers at the tips of the branches. In warm climates it can be evergreen, making it good for pergolas and arches. It is extremely vigorous and is useful for growing among the branches of trees. Like all Tea Roses it has a very long flowering period. It is often seen in old country gardens in all the warmer countries of the world.

Synonym: 'Souvenir de Mme Léonie Viennot'
Classification: Climbing Tea
Breeder: Bernaix, France
Year of introduction: 1897
Parentage: 'Gloire de Dijon' × seedling
Fragrance: Strong
Repeat flowering

'Symphony'

This rose produces compact clusters of plump pink-tinged buds that open to medium-sized, double flowers in a medium yellow, ageing to pink at the edges. The blooms make full, shapely rosettes of up to 45 petals and they are sweetly fragrant. The foliage is mid-green and glossy and the growth is compact, bushy and vigorous. Happiest in warm weather, 'Symphony' is suitable for bed or border.

Codename: AUSlett
Synonym: 'Allux Symphony'
Classification: English Rose
Breeder: Austin, England
Year of introduction: 1986
Parentage: 'The Knight' × 'Yellow Cushion'
Fragrance: Strong
Repeat flowering

'Tamora'

Beautiful apricot flowers are born from rust-colored buds. The flowers are very full and deeply cupped in the Old Garden Rose style. They are medium sized, come in small clusters and have a strong myrrh fragrance. The foliage is small, dark green and semi-glossy and the growth is vigorous and bushy to 1 m (3 ft). It is recommended for warm climates and is useful in borders and in small gardens. It is very disease resistant, but also very thorny.

Codename: AUStamora
Classification: English Rose
Breeder: Austin, England
Year of introduction: 1983
Parentage: 'Chaucer' × 'Conrad Ferdinand Meyer'
Fragrance: Strong
Repeat flowering

'The Reeve'

One of the earlier of the Austins named for characters from *The Canterbury Tales*, it has very cupped flowers in a soft rose pink. The young flowers are balled, with incurved petals, as seen here. It is open and sprawling in growth, making it suitable for cascading downwards in old-fashioned flower arrangements. It is the closest Modern Rose to *Rosa centifolia*, that was so often painted by the Flemish masters. Foliage is rough-textured, dark green and healthy, and the growth habit is suited to trailing over rock walls. It is very resistant to black spot and mildew and has excellent repeat characteristics.

Codename: AUSreeve
Classification: English Rose
Breeder: Austin, England
Year of introduction: 1979
Parentage: 'Lilian Austin' × 'Chaucer'
Fragrance: Strong
Repeat flowering

'Tiffany'

This rose made something of a sensation on its release, winning many awards, including a Gold Medal at Portland in 1954, The All-America Rose Selection in 1955, an American Rose Society award in 1957 and the James Gamble Fragrance Medal in 1962. Long, pointed buds open to large, double, high-centered, very fragrant flowers in a beautiful mix of pink shades, with yellow at the base of the petals. The foliage is dark green and glossy and the growth is vigorous and upright.

Classification: Hybrid Tea
Breeder: Lindquist, USA
Year of introduction: 1954
Parentage: 'Charlotte Armstrong' × 'Girona'
Fragrance: Strong
Repeat flowering

'Tineke'

'Tineke' is one of the best white garden and cut-flower roses, due to its long-lasting flowers, both on the bush and in the vase, where you can expect a week from them. The creamy buds open to very full white flowers of 50–55 petals, which are most attractive at the three-quarter stage, and they hold well from then on. The foliage is rich green and acts as a good fall to the flowers.

Synonym: 'Ines'
Classification: Hybrid Tea
Breeder: Select Roses BV, Holland
Year of introduction: 1989
Parentage: Unknown
Fragrance: None
Repeat flowering

'Touch of Class'

The flowers are coral and cream. They are large, double and of exhibition form, with high centers and a light fragrance. As the blooms age they hold their shape well. Borne on long stems, they are good for the vase. The foliage is large, dark green and semi-glossy and the growth is vigorous, upright and bushy. 'Touch of Class' won the All-America Rose Selection in 1986 and a Gold Medal at Portland in 1988.

Codename: KRIcarlo
Synonym: 'Maréchal le Clerc', 'Marachal Le Clerc'
Classification: Hybrid Tea
Breeder: Kriloff, France
Year of introduction: 1984
Parentage: 'Micäela' × ('Queen Elizabeth' × 'Romantica')
Fragrance: Light
Repeat flowering

'Tournament of Roses'

Named for the centenary of the Pasadena Rose Tournament of Roses, the very warm, salmon pink flowers come in large clusters against very disease-free dark green foliage, with thorny stems. The repeat is quick and abundant, making it an excellent bedding rose for the back of the border or useful as a hedge. Alas, there is no fragrance. 'Tournament of Roses' won the All America Rose Selection in 1989.

Codename: JACient
Synonyms: 'Berkeley', 'Poesie'
Classification: Floribunda
Breeder: Warriner, USA
Year of introduction: 1988
Parentage: 'Impatient' × seedling
Fragrance: None
Repeat flowering

'Troilus'

This rose is named for one of the characters in Shakespeare's *Troilus and Cressida*. The large flowers are a creamy apricot, full of petals and quartered in the style of Old Garden Roses. They come in clusters and are very fragrant. The foliage is large, dark green and semi-glossy and the growth is upright and vigorous to 1.2 m (4 ft). The blooms resemble peonies, and make a good substitute in areas where peonies will not grow. Best in dry climates, the blooms become spotted in wet conditions.

Codename: AUSoil
Classification: English Rose
Breeder: Austin, England
Year of introduction: 1983
Parentage: ('Duchesse de Montebello' ×
    'Chaucer') × 'Charles Austin'
Fragrance: Strong
Repeat flowering

'Twilight Glow'

This is a modern climbing rose that is becoming very popular. It is moderately vigorous (a good characteristic in a climber as it won't get out of control and overrun a pillar or pergola), and has plentiful, glossy green, disease-free foliage. The lightly fragrant flowers are old-fashioned and quartered in a very pleasing shade of apricot. They open flat and the petals are reflexed. Flower production is good right through the rose season.

Codename: MEItosier
Synonyms: 'Lord Byron', 'Polka', 'Polka 91', 'Scented Dawn'
Classification: Climbing Hybrid Tea
Breeder: Meilland, France
Year of introduction: 1991
Parentage: 'Golden Showers' × 'Lichtkönigin Lucia'
Fragrance: Light
Repeat flowering

'Victoriana'

The red-browns, oranges, smoky pinks and grays in this rose are a most unusual combination—there is no other rose quite like it. The strongly fragrant flowers are very full, with a muddled center, on a very short bush, making it ideally suited to grafting as a standard, or for the front of a border. The foliage is plentiful and dark green. 'Victoriana' can be hard to find, as it is hard to propagate, but it is well worth the effort if you like chic and unusual roses.

Classification: Floribunda
Breeder: Le Grice, England
Year of introduction: 1977
Parentage: Unknown
Fragrance: Strong
Repeat flowering

'White Wings'

It can be somewhat hard to find but is included here because it is one of the best single Hybrid Teas, along with its seed parent 'Dainty Bess', and 'Mrs Oakley Fisher'. It is palest pink to off white in color, with a boss of maroon stamens. It is very vigorous in growth, produces many more flowers than 'Dainty Bess' and, if picked in the bud, the blooms last very well in the vase. Foliage is a healthy, leathery green.

Classification: Hybrid Tea
Breeder: Krebs, USA
Year of introduction: 1947
Parentage: 'Dainty Bess' × seedling
Fragrance: Light
Repeat flowering

'Wife of Bath'

This is another from the early series of roses that David Austin named for characters in *The Canterbury Tales*. The large, cupped blooms are full of petals. As the flowers age they become flat and resemble Old Garden Roses. The color is a rich, deep rose pink, fading to blush-pink. There is a light myrrh fragrance. The foliage is small and medium green and the growth is low, bushy and vigorous. 'Wife of Bath' makes a useful contribution to a border and it repeats well.

Codename: AUSbath
Synonym: 'The Wife of Bath'
Classification: English Rose
Breeder: Austin, England
Year of introduction: 1969
Parentage: 'Mme Caroline Testout' ×
    ('Ma Perkins' × 'Constance Spry')
Fragrance: Light
Repeat flowering

'Wild Flower'

This is a charming single rose with creamy yellow flowers that open flat to reveal prominent yellow stamens. In fact, it owes its looks to its grandparent, 'Golden Wings'. It is a pity it does not have the fragrance of that rose. The foliage is dark green and semi-glossy and the growth is below average height and spreading. It tends to be susceptible to fungus diseases, but for those who love single roses, it is well worth growing if you look after it. 'Wild Flower' is useful at the front of the bed or border and if spent blooms are not removed a huge crop of large yellow-orange hips are produced that last for months.

Codename: AUSwing
Synonym: 'Wildflower'
Classification: English Rose
Breeder: Austin, England
Year of introduction: 1986
Parentage: 'Lilian Austin' × ('Canterbury' × 'Golden Wings')
Fragrance: None
Repeat flowering

'Winchester Cathedral'

Originating as a white sport (mutation) of the pink 'Mary Rose', this rose is almost identical, except for the color. Sometimes the white is flushed with pink, or a darker pink streak appears on some of the petals. The flowers are double, very cupped and fragrant. The petals drop rather quickly, but the prolific production of flowers means this rose is spectacular for much of the season. The foliage is medium sized, mid-green and matt and the growth is vigorous, upright and bushy. It is very susceptible to mildew in the autumn—much more so than 'Mary Rose'.

Codename: AUScat
Synonym: 'Winchester'
Classification: English Rose
Breeder: Austin, England
Year of introduction: 1988
Parentage: Sport of 'Mary Rose'
Fragrance: Strong
Repeat flowering

'Windrush'

This is one of the charming semi-double English Roses. The flowers are large, light yellow and very fragrant. The yellow flushes darker towards the centre and the golden stamens are conspicuous. It repeats quickly and produces flowers very freely, making it a delight for the whole season. The foliage is medium sized, mid-green and matt and the growth is very vigorous, disease resistant and branching. Deadheading is recommended to keep up the flower production. Conversely, if the flowers are not removed a good crop of hips is produced.

Codename: AUSrush
Classification: English Rose
Breeder: Austin, England
Year of introduction: 1984
Parentage: Seedling × ('Canterbury' × 'Golden Wings')
Fragrance: Strong
Repeat flowering

'Wise Portia'

Named for the heroine of Shakespeare's *The Merchant of Venice*, this can be a spectacular rose. It bears clusters of large, double, pinkish mauve flowers freely through the season. There is some variation in color, with the best blooms coming in cooler weather, when they are also much larger. Abundant petals and a lush fragrance completes the Old Rose effect. The foliage is dark green and semi-glossy and the growth is bushy; however, it is not the greatest grower and is susceptible to black spot and mildew. But nurture it and take preventive measures for fungus disease and you will be richly rewarded — it really is a wonderful rose.

Codename: AUSport
Classification: English Rose
Breeder: Austin, England
Year of introduction: 1982
Parentage: 'The Knight' × seedling
Fragrance: Strong
Repeat flowering

'Yellow Button'

Introduced in 1975, this is one of the earlier releases of the English Roses and has fallen out of favor in recent years due to its comparatively weak growth and susceptibility to fungus disease. But many people fall in love with it and it is included here for such lovers of novelty. Globular buds open to medium-sized, yellow, quartered flowers, markedly darker in the centre. They do, indeed, resemble yellow buttons and they look well in posies. There is a slight fragrance. The foliage is dark green and the growth is bushy. Preventative treatment for fungus disease is called for and it needs all-round nurturing to perform well.

Codename: AUSlow
Classification: English Rose
Breeder: Austin, England
Year of introduction: 1975
Parentage: 'Wife of Bath' × 'Chinatown'
Fragrance: Slight
Repeat flowering

Index of Alternative Names

KORbin *see* 'Iceberg'
KOResia *see* 'Friesia'
KORikon *see* 'Limelight'
KORlingo *see* 'Kardinal'
KORlita *see* 'Lolita'
KORplasonia *see* 'Our Vanilla'
KORweiso *see* 'Hannah Gordon'
KORwilma *see* 'Perfect Moment'
KRIcarlo *see* 'Touch of Class'
'La Marck' *see* 'Lamarque'
LENip *see* 'Pascali'
litaKOR *see* 'Lolita'
'Lord Byron' *see* 'Twilight Glow'
'Lutin' *see* 'Shady Lady'
MACrexy *see* 'Sexy Rexy'
MACspeego *see* 'Candella'
'Madame de Sombreuil' *see* 'Sombreuil'
'Madame President' *see* 'Madam President'
'Mainzer Fastnacht' *see* 'Blue Moon'
'Marachal Le Clerc' *see* 'Touch of Class'
'Maréchal le Clerc' *see* 'Touch of Class'
'Margaret Merrill' *see* 'Margaret Merril'
'Matilda' *see* 'Seduction'
MEIbeausai *see* 'Seduction'
MEIbil *see* 'Pink Peace'
MEIcesar *see* 'Papa Meilland'
MEIdomonac *see* 'Bonica'
MEIgronura *see* 'Gold Bunny'
MEIhelvet *see* 'Sonia'
MEIlisia *see* 'Princess Margaret of England'
MEIlista *see* 'Princess Margaret of England'
MEImagarmic *see* 'Princess Margaret of England'
MEIrigalu *see* 'Colorama'
MEIsar *see* 'Papa Meilland'
MEIsecaso *see* 'Shady Lady'
MEItosier *see* 'Twilight Glow'
MEIxtraflo *see* 'Shady Lady'
'Mlle de Sombreuil' *see* 'Sombreuil'
'Mme A. Meilland' *see* 'Peace'
'Nuage Parfumé' *see* 'Fragrant Cloud'
'Pearl of Bedfordview' *see* 'Seduction'
'Peccato di Giola' *see* 'Joyfulness'
'Poesie' see 'Tournament of Roses
'Polka 91' *see* 'Twilight Glow'
'Polka' *see* 'Twilight Glow'
POUmidor *see* 'Royal Dane'

'Preference' *see* 'Princesse de Monaco'
'Premier Amour' *see* 'First Love'
'Princess of Monaco' *see* 'Princesse de Monaco'
'Princesse Grace de Monaco' *see* 'Princesse de Monaco'
'Princesse Grace' *see* 'Princesse de Monaco'
'Princesse Margaret d'Angleterre' *see* 'Princess Margaret of England'
'Queen of Beauty and Fragrance' *see* 'Souvenir de la Malmaison'
'Queen of England' *see* 'Queen Elizabeth'
R. r. 'Superba' *see* 'Scabrosa'
R. turkestanica see 'Mutabilis'
'Raspberry Ice' *see* 'Hannah Gordon'
'Redgold' *see* 'Red Gold'
'Rimosa '79' *see* 'Gold Bunny'
'Roberta' *see* 'Heritage'
Rosa chinensis mutabilis see 'Mutabilis'
Rosa gallica complicata see 'Complicata'
Rosa rugosa scabrosa see 'Scabrosa'
'Rouge et Or' *see* 'Red Gold'
'Scented Dawn' *see* 'Twilight Glow'
'Schneewittchen' *see* 'Iceberg'
'Sharifa' see 'Sharifa Asma'
'Sissi' *see* 'Blue Moon'
'Sonia Meilland' *see* 'Sonia'
'Souvenir d'Elisa Vardon' *see* 'Souvenir d'Elise Vardon'
'Souvenir de Mme Léonie Viennot' *see* 'Souvenir de Mme Léonnie Viennot'
'St Cecelia' *see* 'St Cecilia'
'Sunsprite' *see* 'Friesia'
'Sweet Promise' *see* 'Sonia'
TANellis *see* 'Fragrant Cloud'
TANnacht *see* 'Blue Moon'
TANsinnroh *see* 'Joyfulness'
'Thé Maréchal' *see* 'Lamarque'
'The New Dawn' *see* 'New Dawn'
'The Queen Elizabeth Rose' *see* 'Queen Elizabeth'
'Tipo Idéale' *see* 'Mutabilis'
'Troika' *see* 'Royal Dane'
'Vanilla' *see* 'Our Vanilla'
WEKamanda *see* 'St Patrick'
WEZeip *see* 'Paradise'
'Wildflower' *see* 'Wild Flower'
'Winchester' *see* 'Winchester Cathedral'